The State of Black Girls

The go-to guide for creating safe spaces for Black girls.

By Marline Francois-Madden, LCSW

Written by Marline Francois-Madden
Edited by Kim-Lee Patterson
Cover by 99Designs
Back cover photography by Dexterity Productions

ISBN: 978-0-578-49515-6

www.thestateofblackgirls.com

Printed in the United States of America

Dedication

I dedicate this book to every Black girl who feels invisible and misunderstood by people in this world. The goal is to help you recognize your voice needs to be heard. You will find strategies and tools to help you navigate each phase and chapter of your life. This is for you, your sister, your cousin, your best friend, the younger version of you, and for every Black girl, because all of you matter.

Table of Contents

Introduction

On December 15, 2018, I read the story of a 9-year-old girl who died by suicide after dealing with bullies at her school. That left me feeling heartbroken, frustrated and hopeless. Countless stories of young girls who deal with depression, suicidal ideations, anxiety, abuse, etc. moved me to do more aside from seeing clients in my therapy practice.

I knew I needed to give young girls an outlet to hear about mental health without feeling ashamed. I wanted girls to know that they were not alone. The more I worked in my practice, the more I realized that Black girls needed their voices to be heard. This book was birthed from my pain and many frustrations with the lack of safe spaces for Black girls.

This book is for every Black girl and her parents, educators, community organizers, and policy makers. This book is divided into various topics with segments for Black girls along with guided activities and resources. The purpose of this book is to bring awareness and change to ensure the voices of Black girls are heard. We are sick and tired of the disparities and challenges Black girls face. Remember, this book does not substitute for therapeutic services.

Chapter 1: Do Black Girls Really Matter?

Dear Black Girl,

The world will make you feel like you don't matter. I want you to know that, no matter what society, the media, and your community says, you *do* matter. The media always tries to portray Black girls as angry, loud, aggressive, and ratchet.

A study conducted by Georgetown University reported that people even view Black girls as being less innocent than white girls (Epstein, et al.). No matter what the world thinks about you, I want you to believe that you matter. You were created for a special purpose and you have a mission to accomplish while you are here on earth.

Sometimes, we seek validation from other people and believe what they think about us. It is time you look within for validation and be bold in your confidence. As you grow and blossom in this world, you will navigate various spaces, such as at school, with your peers or family, and through society.

Sometimes, being a Black girl can become extremely stressful, especially when you are not given the same opportunities as white girls, or when people form negative perceptions of who you are without getting to know you.

I wrote this book for you, for your friends, your sister and cousins, your bestie, and your squad. This book was created for you to have a space where you belong and can find the helpful tools and strategies I offer as a licensed teen psychotherapist.

As you journey through each chapter, I want you to know that I hear, see and value you. I appreciate you for your uniqueness. I want your voice to be heard, loud and clear, throughout this book. Even when your voice shakes, speak up and show up in your most authentic way.

Your voice matters in this world. When this world tries to discredit you, just link arms with your sisters and show them that Black girls *do* matter.

Throughout this book, you will find lists of activities to do. You can do these activities alone or with a group of girlfriends. So, let's get started with the first activity.

Black Girls Matter Activity

Write a list of 10 reasons why Black girls matter.

1. Black Girls Matter because_____

2. Black Girls Matter because_____

3. Black Girls Matter because_____

4. Black Girls Matter because_____

5. Black Girls Matter because_____

6. Black Girls Matter because_____

7. Black Girls Matter because_____

8. Black Girls Matter because_____

9. Black Girls Matter because_____

10. Black Girls Matter because_____

Thought Questions

How did you feel completing this assignment?

Did you struggle to complete this assignment?

If so, ask friends or family to help you complete it.

Remember this: even when the world doubts you, you

matter and have value in this world.

Chapter 2:

Self-Esteem, Selfies and Identity

Dear Black Girl,

You are beautiful inside and out. I know we live in a world where many compare themselves to others in magazines, in the media, and on social media. You'd be surprised to know how many teens I meet who struggle with their self-esteem. Many find it hard to identify just 3 things that they like about themselves. From hair texture to skin color to body image, it is easy to feel like you are not perfect.

If you get caught up in looking what the world defines as beautiful, you may start to feel as if you don't have it all together. In the world of social media, it is easy to start comparing yourself to others and become anxious about how you are viewed by society. Societal pressures will try make you feel like you are not good or pretty enough as who you were created to be.

During my high school years, I thought my identity was measured by having nice things, like buying new sneakers or having my hair nicely done regularly. I remember spending entire paychecks to have the latest fashion trends, just so I could fit in with the popular crowd. I wanted to hear others say "OMG, you look so cute!"

Sometimes, we allow others to shape our self-esteem and determine what it should look like. It's easy to get caught up in the rat race, wanting to hear the "YASSSSS" from your friends and others, whether in person or in your Instagram comments. As a Black girl, your experience with your identity will be different from what a white girl would experience. You may face challenges with how people view you because of your hair texture, skin color, and body type. You live in a world that constantly tries to put a label on what being "pretty for a Black girl" looks like. That can be stressful.

Let's Talk About Hair Textures

I remember when having relaxed hair was the way our hair needed to be. People even told me, "your hair looks nappy." Now, there is a decrease in the sales of relaxers and more Black women are investing in natural hair care products and options. Whether you're wearing a lace front, your edges are laid, your braids are on point, or your twist out is flourishing, I want you to *own* it and feel beautiful.

Sometimes, other people may not understand your hair texture and will want to touch your hair. If you don't feel comfortable with someone touching your hair, you have every right to say no. Your hair is a part of who you are. You can set boundaries for who gets to touch it.

When it comes to your hair, don't compare your hair texture to what other Black and brown girls have. Just because someone else has looser curls does not mean that your tight curls don't matter—and vice versa. Hair textures range from 1a-4c. The higher the number, the tighter the curls are.

Take time to learn about your hair texture and how to properly maintain it and keep it healthy. That could mean greasing your scalp, getting your hair trimmed, not leaving your braids in longer than expected and remembering to drink water and take your vitamins.

Let's Talk Skin Color

I remember when I was in college, I used to hear the "light skin" versus "dark skin" conversation happening all around school. The guys even created a private group just for the light-skinned girls and this started a mini-war between all the girls on campus.

Society really wants us to not get along, but you can break that stereotype. For so long, society has ingrained in us the idea that "lighter is better" by being selective with who represents the entire Black girl community on their magazine covers, TV commercials and in fashion shows.

Lately, there has been a shift in the culture. There is more representation of Black girls in the media. Barbie Dolls now exist with natural hair and various skin tones. There are more Black-owned beauty products and a larger representation of Black girls who look like us on TV, in movies, and in fashion campaigns and ads, etc. The narrative is shifting, yes, but there is still a deep-rooted issue regarding colorism.

Maybe you've heard statements like "you're pretty for a dark skin girl" or "you must be mixed with something." You never want people to put a measure to your worth based on your skin color. It doesn't matter what complexion you identify with as a Black girl—you still matter.

Let's Talk About Body Image

Girls often talk about things they want to change about their body features, whether it's their height, weight, birthmarks, special features, etc. Statistics show that 44% of girls try to lose weight in high school and 7 in 10 girls feel like they aren't good enough or don't measure up in some way ("11

Facts About Teens and Self Esteem"). When you see these statistics, I want you to know that you are not alone. There is a chance that your friends are going through similar experiences. Sometimes, girls struggle with their weight and feel self-conscious about their outfit selections.

If you struggle with self-esteem, there are ways to boost your self-confidence. Boosting your self-esteem is not about using filters, makeup, and highlights. It is an internal feeling. You must feel good in who you were created to be.

Your self-esteem should not be connected to how much others validate you, but how you are able to define and validate yourself. There are several ways you can boost your self-esteem, including by affirming yourself, perfecting your skills and talents, and volunteering in your local community.

Self-Esteem Journaling Activity

Write a positive letter of affirmation to yourself here or in a journal.

_____

_____

_____

_____

_____

_____

_____

_____

_____

_____

_____

_____

_____

_____

_____

_____

_____

_____

_____

Thought Questions

Do you feel like you have good self-esteem?

How do you identify how you feel about yourself?

Who shaped your idea of what beauty is? Where?

List the characteristics and traits you recognize in yourself.

List the positive characteristics family/friends see in you.

If there is something you want to change about yourself, I want you to start viewing it as unique.

Chapter 3: Social Media

Dear Black Girl,

Instagram, Snapchat, Facebook, and YouTube—you probably have all these apps on your cell phone. It can be a good and bad thing to have access to social media. I am sure you've probably heard adults saying, "Why are you always on your phone?"

Sometimes people don't realize that your online community are your friends. You love to connect and engage with them through the screen. It can be frustrating to feel like you can't be on your phone with your friends. Yes, I get it, you want to connect, but let's talk about some of the challenges with being on social media.

One recurring struggle I see with teens using these apps is that they end up feeling like other people have better lives than they do because of what they see being posted online. At times, it may feel like what you see online is the standard of beauty, especially in determining what is "pretty for a Black girl."

Social media tends to make some people feel stressed out after scrolling through the apps. Do you find yourself comparing yourself to others on social media or feeling like you don't have enough likes or friends compared to other people at your school? Are you trying to be popular by taking 1,000 selfies just to find the best one to post on social media?

Teenagers today have more struggles with depression, anxiety, loneliness, and self-esteem than their parents and grandparents did. Heavy use of social media can impact your mental health. You may find it hard to express your feelings and emotions at times and turn to social media to express how you're feeling with people in your online community.

It may feel like your friends don't have a clue what you're dealing with because of what you post on social media. Perhaps you post funny memes and pictures but, deep down inside, you feel sad, depressed and lonely. Maybe you are extremely upset about an old friend who found a new bestie to hang out with and feel like you've lost your friend.

Social media can bring on a wide range of emotions; even over the span of a single day. Let me share a secret with you: social media is not real life. You only see snippets of the life of others on the platform. People can post their relationship goals on Instagram, but you have no idea about the 30-minute argument they had right before they posted the picture.

Don't allow the pictures that people post on social media to create any feelings of anger, resentment, jealousy, or loneliness. Set boundaries on social media if you are developing unhealthy behaviors or emotional patterns while on the platforms. Don't allow yourself to overuse social media so much that you neglect to connect with those around you or complete your homework assignments.

Do's and Don'ts of Social Media

- Do set boundaries and limit the time you spend online.

- Do not take nudes or send nudes to others on social media (yes, I said don't do it).

- Do keep your page private and be careful of who you're adding and who is following your page.

- Do never share or post your location on social media—even after you have left the place.

- Do take social media breaks when you feel anxious, depressed, overwhelmed or angered by something that happened on social media.

- Don't send subliminal messages on social media.

- Don't screenshot private DMs to share with other friends and create drama.

- Don't vent about things you should share with a trusted peer, mentor or parent on social media.

- Don't post inappropriate things on the app. If you don't want your parents to see it, don't post it.

Social Media Activity

Assess how much time you have spent on social media each day.

Make a conscious decision to decrease your daily social media usage and focus that extra time on learning a new hobby, spending time with your family, finishing your homework or mastering your skills.

You can get someone to help you with this challenge. Record your progress on what you are doing with your time rather than being on social media.

Chapter 4:

Sisterhood, Friendships, Forgiveness

Dear Black Girl,

I want to share a story about my sisterhood and friendship journey with you. My best friend and I are two days apart and have been friends since we were born. We have celebrated so many childhood birthdays and precious moments together. I have other girlfriends too, who I've been friends with since my childhood years. They have taught me the benefits of having friendships with other women.

When I was 8 years old, my mother taught me the principles of building healthy friendships with other girls and not chasing after the hype. Eventually, though, the moment came where I tried to chase after that hype. I wanted to hang out with the popular girls in middle school.

It wasn't long before I realized that I ghosted all my old friends just to hang out with these other girls. Those popular girls started talking about my friends and it was very uncomfortable for me to sit there and listen to the bashing. In that moment, I chose to end my friendship with them, and I returned to my old friends.

I remember hearing girls say, "I don't hang out with other girls because they start drama" and I would cringe, wondering why these girls didn't have any girlfriends. Sisterhood is a beautiful thing. You can create healthy friendships with other girls and thrive. You don't have to fall victim to the name-calling, gossiping, and subliminal messages you see other girls post on social media. You can build a solid friendship with other girls.

The purpose of sisterhood is to keep friends who have your back and speak on your behalf, even when you are not in the room. Your friends should not gossip about you or to you about other people. One of the joys of being in a trusted sisterhood is having a tribe you can talk to when you're going through a rough time. Another is having them there to help you glow up.

Your friends should challenge you daily to be a better you. So many reality shows portray Black women arguing with one another, but this is not an accurate view of what sisterhood looks like. This narrative does not have to be your story. You can work towards building your tribe.

Conflict among teen girls can be a difficult space to navigate. Maybe you and your friend are having trouble maintaining your friendship. Suddenly, you are stuck between faking the friendship and cutting her loose.

Perhaps letting go of the friendship will leave you stuck and forced to decide on how you will hang out with other friends in the same circle. Between the group chats and shared classes, it can be hard to let go of a friendship. You spend most of your days with them in school, trying to maintain the balance of being a nice friend.

Perhaps you need to evaluate yourself and see if you are being a good friend or not. Are you the one throwing shade at your friends for keeping their friendship with that one girl you don't get along with in school?

If you have a friendship that is struggling, process how you feel and how you can make changes to restore the friendship. Often, teenagers will get upset with friends and move on to the next friend group without ever discussing a conflict resolution. Ask yourself if you are dealing with hurt, rejection, heartbreak, and anger from a friendship that fell apart.

Don't let your pride get in the way of you rebuilding a friendship that you once enjoyed. I do understand that there are times where you and your friend will grow apart. You will recognize when a relationship is not worth keeping. There is an activity in this book to help you to identify which friendships are worth keeping or saying goodbye to.

Conflicts, disagreements, and confrontations are hard to deal with in a healthy manner in high school sometimes.

Do you ever find yourself avoiding your friends just because you don't want to start anymore drama with them? Remember, friendships are like building a community. You will have to assess whether the friendship is for you and if you are displaying the qualities of a good friend yourself.

It's easy to get caught up in how badly our friends hurt our feelings or made us upset without ever stopping to think about what you have done to affect the friendship too. Ask yourself if your friends can trust you. Are you reliable when they are in need? Friendship is supposed to be a two-way street.

Once you have decided that a friendship is mutually beneficial, you will need to learn how to develop and grow a healthy friendship with your friend. One way to grow and keep healthy friendships is by showing up when they need you most. So often we tend to neglect our friends in those moments when they need us to be there.

When I say show up, I don't just mean by displaying sympathy for her on the day she tells you that she broke up with her man. Showing up is following up with her about a goal she told you about several weeks ago or asking her how her ill grandmother is doing and how you can emotionally support her during this time.

How would you feel if no one was checking in on you to see how you were doing, or if no one showed up when you needed them most? This is a great place to start in establishing a trusting relationship with your friend.

Another way to build healthy friendships is by learning how to forgive. Forgiveness is a very difficult thing for many people to do and it is easy to hold grudges for a long time. When you decide to forgive your friend for whatever they have done to hurt you, it is up to you to move forward and not bring it up in the future.

Sisterhood Journaling Activity, Part 1

Write a positive letter to one of your close friends about how much you value the friendship.

Also, consider asking one of your friends to write a positive letter to you about why the friendship is important to them. If you are feeling stuck on this activity, consider doing the next activity. That will give you some guidance.

Sisterhood Journal Activity, Part 2

Who are your best friends?

List some of the reasons why they are your best friends.

What are some qualities you look for in a friendship?

Why do people enjoy being friends with you?

Do you have a friendship that fell off?

Who do you need to forgive?

Consider writing a letter of apology or forgiveness to practice what you will say to them.

Chapter 5: Do Black Girls Go to Therapy?

Dear Black Girl,

Growing up, I always knew I wanted to be a therapist, but I had never considered going to see one. I did not think therapy was something for me. I assumed it was only for the people I saw on TV or people who heard voices and had schizophrenia. Many teen magazines had a section called "Ask the Therapist" and I would visualize my life as a therapist as I read them. The older I got, the more I recognized that I also needed therapy to address the childhood traumas that impacted my relationships. It took me nearly two years to make a call to a therapist, but I am so glad that I did and went to my first therapy session. It can be nerve-wrecking and a bit scary to think that you need to see a therapist, especially on the journey to becoming one yourself. My therapist was also a Black woman, so I felt extremely comfortable talking about growing up in a Haitian household.

Do Black girls go to therapy? Yes, they do. There is a stigma surrounding mental illness and those who seek therapy services, but you can help to dismantle some of these myths. Seeing a therapist can give you a space to express your thoughts and feelings.

Many often think that seeing a therapist means that you must be "crazy," but I'd like for you to remove the word crazy from your vocabulary. Therapy gives you an outlet to explore your internal battles and create a roadmap to address the barriers and stressors in your life. There are times when you may want to see a therapist but feel embarrassed to seek help.

I have heard stories from teens who were interested in seeing a therapist but feared that their parents would go against their decision. In these cases, the teen ends up suffering in silence and never addressing their current stressors. So, what happens when you finally do go to therapy? Therapy is meant to be your safe space to explore your thoughts, feelings, and behaviors.

Your therapist's job is to keep everything said during your session confidential, unless you are in imminent risk or danger and/or express suicidal thoughts. You will work with your therapist to identify your reasons for going to therapy and the goals you would like to work on. Just because you go to therapy does not mean you have a mental illness.

Therapy is a great investment for your mental health. In my many years of working as a therapist, I have seen many teens express how therapy has helped them learn how to manage their emotions better and use statements such as "I feel." Therapy can create opportunities for growth and self-awareness, but it also requires some work on your part to participate in the process. There will be times when your therapist will assign homework and exercises for you to practice during the week. These assignments are designed to help you to put into practice what you've learned in therapy and to analyze your progress. If you would like to see a therapist, talk to your parents about why you want to see one. They can help you schedule your first therapy session and even attend the first session with you, to get to know the therapist. As you begin to navigate this new journey, I want you to be open to the process and not allow fear to hinder your ability to seek help when you need it.

Resources:

Where to Find a Therapist?

- www.therapyforblackgirls.com

- www.psychologytoday.com

- www.goodtherapy.com

- www.therapyforblackmen.org

Mental Health Apps for Teens

- NotOK App

- Mindshift

- Calm App

- HeadSpace

Chapter 6:

The Anxious Brain

"I Have Too Much on My Mind"

Dear Black Girl,

Your paper is due tomorrow morning and you're still writing the introduction. Your room is a mess, the dishes are still in the sink. You promised your sister you'd hang out with her, yet you've spent the last 4 hours Facetiming your bestie. I know—it felt good to talk with your bestie. After all, you only have one class together and you needed to catch up on the day-to-day events in school.

It's 9:54 p.m. when you open your laptop and start to feel anxious about your paper. Your heart beats faster, your thoughts race, and you're feeling more worried about this assignment. Maybe you say, "what's the point in doing this paper? It won't be good enough at this point anyway." You feel discouraged from trying to get your assignments done, so you shut your bedroom door and start crying.

Perhaps your mother has no idea what you're dealing with in school and you struggle to tell her about your assignments. You feel even more anxious as you start to think about the amount of time you have left to complete this assignment. You're currently pulling a D in this class. The more you try to do your work, the more your heart races and your palms sweat.

You're already tired, but now you're feeling fatigued. You tell yourself, "That's it! I am not doing this assignment." You shut the book and place it in your book bag, saying, "Whew! I'm going to bed!" Hours later, you wake up feeling anxious. Your stomach hurts and you tell your mom that you don't feel like going to school today.

Sometimes, when you are feeling anxious, you may feel the need to not attend school. However, this only pacifies the anxiety for a short period of time. The longer you avoid anxiety, the more it is prolonged. What would you say if I told you that 25.1% of teens age 13-18 suffer with anxiety? (*Anxiety and Depression Association of America*) This just means it's more common than you think.

Anxiety is a treatable disorder, so you can learn the skills and tools to help sooth your moments of anxiety. When you're feeling anxious, you may start to avoid people, places, and things. Sometimes you may not want to have "that feeling," you know… feelings of sadness or moments when you cry.

Anxiety can lead to panic attacks at school, which are difficult and may make you want to run to the nurse's office. Please know that you are not alone. Many teenagers deal with anxiety. Symptoms of anxiety include shortness of breath, a racing heartbeat that is faster than usual, restlessness, and insomnia.

You might find that you're easily distracted and can't focus, or that you are worrying too much about things that have not or will never happen. Your palms may feel sweaty and you can feel like there is literally so much going on in your mind.

Even if you identify with many of these symptoms, remember that you can't diagnose yourself. You will need to see a licensed mental health professional or medical practitioner to get a formal diagnosis of anxiety. On the next page, you will find some tips and activities to help you navigate your moments of anxiety.

Anxiety Guided Activity

Can you identify when you feel the most anxious?

Write down your top 5 stressors.

1. _____

2. _____

3. _____

4. _____

5. _____

Write down the 5 things that makes you feel calm?

1. _____

2. _____

3. _____

4. _____

5. _____

Below are activities you can do to decrease your stressors.

- Exercise.

- Do yoga.

- Talk to a trusted friend.

- Laugh.

- Cry.

- Journal your thoughts.

- Take a nap.

- Talk to a parent or trusted adult figure.

- Talk to your therapist or school counselor.

- Listen to music.

- Download a meditation app (e.g. Headspace).

- Dance.

- Paint or draw.

- Practice some deep breathing exercises.

Here is a deep breathing exercise you can practice:

Inhale for 5 seconds through your nose with your mouth closed, and then exhale for 5 seconds through your open mouth. You can repeat this several times and practice this throughout the day.

Chapter 7: Am I Depressed?

Dear Black Girl,

Do you know when you feel depressed or sad? Sometimes, you may feel alone and like no one understands what you are going through. Depression can look different in teen girls. Sometimes you might feel hopeless, irritable, little motivation and no desire to hang out with your friends. You might be easily distracted and struggle to get out of the funk you are in.

Remember, feeling sad does not necessarily mean you are depressed. Depression is a clinical diagnosis and usually impairs your daily life activities, whereas sadness can be short-lived and caused by a specific situation. Studies have shown that nearly 1/4 of teenage girls suffer from depression (Girls and Teens | Anxiety and Depression Association of America, ADAA).

Maybe you aren't depressed, but you hear your friends talk about how depressed they feel. Do you say to yourself, "but she's always so happy! There's no way she's depressed!" Sometimes, people can wear a smile on their face, but be depressed and suffering inside in silence.

Maybe you are the girl who smiles at school with your friends, only to come home and lock yourself in your room crying all night. Perhaps you feel like your family doesn't understand you and they tell you that you have no reason to be sad.

When you feel like no one cares about you, being in your room can feel like an escape and a way to isolate from people. You may even want to tell your parents what you're dealing with but feel like they may panic or tell you that you don't have depression.

Maybe you don't want to tell your parents because you feel like they are already dealing with enough stress. It is hard to deal with depression and sadness on your own. You will need supportive people around you. I hear you, and I know it's hard. Escaping can be seen as a form of isolation.

Isolation is one of the symptoms of depression and it can be hard to express those feelings to other people. As a Black girl, you may have faced so many challenges and seen the headlines showing what people think of Black girls. Have you ever felt like people dismissed how you felt, and you didn't have anyone to talk to? When you are feeling depressed, ask yourself what is triggering you at that moment.

At times, you may feel completely alone and like no one understands how you feel every day. Sometimes it seems hard to find a safe outlet to talk about how you feel. When you or someone you know is feeling depressed, it may feel like a good idea to isolate yourself. Some form coping skills that are negative.

This chapter will provide some guided activities to help you engage in a list of positive coping skills.

Questions to Ask & Guided Activity

What happens when you feel suicidal and alone?

Do you have anyone to go to?

Write down a list of things that makes you feel depressed.

What are your thoughts telling you at this moment?

How does your body feel physically?

Write down at least 3-5 people who can be your support system when you feel depressed.

What are your triggers?

If you are feeling suicidal, call the hotline number 1-800-273-8255.

Journaling Activity

Identify your thoughts and feelings by practicing writing

down how you feel on this page or in a journal.

_____

_____

_____

_____

_____

_____

_____

_____

_____

_____

Write a positive letter to yourself or ask a friend to write a positive letter about you here.

_____

_____

_____

_____

_____

_____

_____

_____

_____

_____

_____

_____

_____

_____

This chapter includes a section for parents as depression and suicide are areas that adults should pay attention to.

Dear Parents,

It can be difficult to hear that your teenage daughter is dealing with depression, and even harder to figure out what to do next. Have you tried talking to your daughter but felt like you were unsure of what to say or do? Maybe you feel afraid of what will happen and have anxiously looked up resources on the Internet on how to help your daughter.

Perhaps, you have heard stories from another friend who has a daughter going through depression and you fear that your daughter may end up going downhill from here. Maybe you've even begun looking for a therapist within your community or an organization that can assist her but can't seem to find the right program for her.

During this time, support your daughter. Look out for warning signs, such as isolation, a change in her appetite, irritability, lack of interest in hanging out with her friends or doing activities she once enjoyed. Keep an eye out for physical and emotional symptoms, too. Consider joining a support group to help your daughter during this difficult time.

Remember, even if you don't understand why she feels depressed, I want you to use this opportunity to connect with your daughter and help her feel supported by you. According to the National Institute of Mental Health, depression is a medical illness that can interfere with your ability to handle your daily activities, such as sleeping, eating, or doing schoolwork.

Often, adults can misdiagnose teens and not recognize the signs of depression for what they are. One of the symptoms of depression in teens that looks different from an adult diagnosis is irritability. Depression is a common mental health diagnosis among teens and can be treated with professional help.

Some of the most common treatment approaches is the use of psychotherapy and/or antidepressant medications as prescribed by a psychiatrist or medical doctor. Psychotherapy (also known as "talk therapy") is a way for your daughter to talk to a licensed mental health professional about her thoughts and feelings.

Psychotherapy allows her to identify her triggers and develop coping strategies to manage her emotions. If your daughter expresses thoughts of harming herself, a therapist will work with her to develop a safety plan and assess the risk of danger. Parents often ask, "Does my daughter need medications for depression too?" The discussion of medication will warrant a visit to a psychiatrist who will determine if your daughter needs medications.

A therapist cannot prescribe medications or modify the dosage of the psychotropics your daughter is on. A psychiatrist will manage and monitor these medications and determine the dosage and frequency. You know your daughter better than anyone else does, so observe her closely and monitor her behaviors—and whether she is taking her medications.

Aside from medication and therapy, you may want to investigate other resources to help yourself as a parent. These include parent support groups, family therapy, mental health first aid workshops, or individual therapy. The more knowledgeable you are about the diagnosis, the more prepared you will be to advocate for your daughter and find support for yourself when it gets overwhelming.

Chapter 8: Self-Harm

"Self-harm is not the same as suicide"

Dear Black Girl,

This chapter may contain triggering words or topics, so please read with caution. If you find this chapter to be extremely intense, then I want you to pause and consider skipping it. Perhaps, you can ask an adult (like a parent or your therapist) to read this chapter first to make sure it is age-appropriate and suitable for you. I will talk about the challenges that Black girls who practice self-harm face and provide helpful tips and strategies to deal with self-harm.

Remember self-harm and suicidal thoughts are not the same thing. One may have the urge to self-harm, but never express suicidal ideation or plans to die. Many people used to think that self-harm (also known as cutting) was a white girl problem. However, with the growing rates of depression among youths in the Black community, this is becoming an issue within our own communities as well.

I have seen parents panic when they recognize a cut or wounds on their daughter's body. It is completely natural to experience this. If you are a teen struggling with self-harm, I want you to know that there is help available to get you through this. I have heard teens talk about experiencing emotional pain they couldn't explain.

By engaging in self-harm, they felt it was a way to recognize that they were "real" and "alive" through experiencing physical pain. For some teens who self-harm, this behavior causes some relief, but it is an unhealthy coping strategy to deal with their thoughts, feelings, and emotions.

My goal is to teach girls to identify their triggers and then find strategies to reduce their stressors without engaging in unhealthy patterns. Of course, reading this does not replace seeing a therapist. I want you to take an inventory of the unhealthy patterns you have and then think about how you can replace them with positive patterns.

A few things you can do include journaling, singing, dancing, working out, meditating, and deep breathing. You can also place a rubber-band around your wrist and snap the rubber-band whenever you want to feel present in the moment. Another positive practice to try is holding ice in your hand, to help bring the feeling to your palm, and then letting go of the ice.

You can work with your therapist to learn new mindfulness practices to incorporate in your day-to-day life when you start to feel stressed out. Remember to be open and honest with a parent and/or counselor when you experience self-harm behaviors. This is not an easy journey and many parents struggle to help their daughters address this issue. It is okay to get help and work through the process of healing.

Chapter 9:

I Was Sexually Abused, and No One

Knows

Dear Black Girl,

This chapter may be painful to read, and you may be triggered to remember what happened to you. I want you to take a deep breath in and then release it. You are still here, and you are valuable. Sexual abuse is extremely difficult to go through. Trust me: I know very well.

Between 8-11 years old, I experienced sexual abuse too. Maybe you feel confused and don't know what to do. Maybe you are holding this secret in because you fear what your family may say. It is even harder to experience sexual abuse when it is someone that you know or who is close to your family.

Did you know that most people who experience sexual abuse know their abusers? It's such a hard space to be in. Maybe you have flashbacks, nightmares or a hard time trusting anyone because of what you've been through. I want you to know that you are not alone. There are other Black girls and women who have experienced sexual abuse too.

Whether you are a victim of rape, molestation, assault, or incest, I want you to know that you can move forward and live beyond the trauma you've experienced. You are a SURVIVOR! I know the abuse makes you feel ashamed or guilty; maybe you are not in the mood to talk about it with others. Maybe you feel like pushing it under the rug.

I want to speak to you about how trauma impacts your life. When you've dealt with sexual abuse, please recognize that you have experienced a form of trauma. Trauma can make you feel on edge and on alert, wanting to protect yourself from future harm. At times, trauma makes you forget what happened. It may feel like you have amnesia.

There are some psychological effects that occur when you experience trauma, such as dissociation. Some people struggle with memory recall during traumatic events. Sexual abuse is a traumatic event that can cause you to not remember important dates, special occasions, or a certain time period in your life, etc.

I have spoken to many girls who were survivors of sexual abuse who don't remember some of their school years or social gatherings they attended during the years that they experienced abuse. Sometimes, they go through cycles where they suddenly remember the abuse that occurred, and it is very difficult for them to manage their thoughts and emotions in that moment.

When you can't recall a traumatic event, you may find yourself remembering what happened out of nowhere. This could be triggered by a sound, smell, taste, environment, etc. that reminds your brain of the trauma. It may link it to your abuse history and make you feel like you are experiencing it all over again.

When you are triggered, you may start to feel anxious and guarded. You may experience nightmares and flashbacks, guilt, shame, and even confusion. If you find yourself experiencing some of these symptoms, I want you to seek help and speak out about your trauma. If you've followed the #MeToo movement by Tarana Burke, then you are fully aware of the silenced stories of Black girls all over the world who have experienced sexual violence and assault at the hands of a perpetrator.

For so long, Black girls were told to be quiet or that no one would believe their stories. I remember what it was like being 11 years old and making the decision that I was not going to be in the presence of my abuser again. I remember feeling confused and angry, asking "How could this happen to me?" My parents had no idea that I was sexually molested by a relative until my adulthood. I felt embarrassed and ashamed to disclose what happened, in fear of getting in trouble.

As I got older, I recognized that I wasn't the only person who kept silent year after year about their abuse. One study related to disclosure says that only 38% of child abuse victims will speak about their sexual abuse (*Child Abuse Statistics*). So, imagine how many girls have not disclosed their abuse. Another thing you must recognize is this: when a Black girl experiences sexual abuse, it is not her fault. She is not the cause of her abuse. She was violated and taken advantage of by someone else.

Despite the large number of survivors who remain silent, you now live in an era where people are speaking up about their abuse. However, it can also be triggering to follow on social media. What happens if you or someone you know is dealing with abuse? You'll want to find a trusted person and let them know what you have dealt with. Let them help you figure out how to feel safe and where to get the help you will need to deal with the trauma.

So, how do you begin to heal from sexual abuse? You start by getting real with your thoughts and feelings. Talk about what you've experienced with someone you trust. It can be difficult to openly share what happened with anyone, so consider talking to a therapist. There are many therapists who are clinically trained in treating girls who have experienced trauma or have a complexity of trauma. We know that trauma shows up differently for girls of color. That is why there are therapists who are not only trained in trauma treatment but are also culturally competent to address cultural and racial barriers.

If you or someone you know has experienced sexual abuse, a therapist can help you to learn how to cope with the stressors and triggers related to the abuse. A therapist may suggest that you do a psychological assessment, individual therapy, group therapy, trauma therapy, etc., to help you heal. Therapy is often stigmatized in many Black communities, but this may help you to address any traumatic experiences.

Aside from psychotherapy, consider other resources where you can find communities of other trusted individuals or ways to advocate for other girls who may have experienced sexual abuse. There are various support groups, hotlines, workshops, and advocacy groups both throughout the United States and internationally that work with girls to provide them resources beyond those that address your therapeutic needs.

Advocacy can really help you to speak out about an issue that affects millions of girls throughout the world and in countries where girls are often silenced or ridiculed for experiencing sexual abuse. Experiencing sexual abuse is painful. Using the many resources available, you can develop a passion for helping others through their journey of healing.

I was once that 11-year-old girl who was silenced about her abuse. Now, I run wellness programs throughout the world to give Black girls the skills and tools they need to address their mental health.

Resources

Darkness 2 Light:

www.d2l.org

Rape, Abuse, and Incest National Network:

www.rainn.org

The National Child Traumatic Stress Network:

www.nctsn.org

Chapter 10: Grief and Loss

Dear Black Girl,

Grief is inevitable. It happens to everyone in different forms. When we are faced with grief, it can be difficult to learn how to cope with and process the loss. Grief and loss can occur in many ways, such as losing a loved one or a pet, or experiencing unexpected and sudden changes, like tearing your ACL while playing basketball or seeing a parent get incarcerated. You may feel unprepared when these things happen and struggle to manage the emotions that follow the loss.

I have had multiple losses in my life, but one of the most difficult ones was having my grandmother passed away the summer after my sophomore year in college. My grandmother always had health challenges, but she lived on her own and was independent. One day, she went into the hospital and she never returned home. Things went from one health issue to the doctors installing a feeding tube and eventually, placing her on life support. My grandmother began to have memory recall issues, too.

One day, I called my parents while they were visiting my grandmother at the hospital and asked, "How is grandma doing?" My mom responded in a low-toned voice, "We will talk when we get home." I knew something was up and started to feel anxious as I waited for my parents to return home. When they did, I could tell something was up just from the dry looks on their faces. They felt hopeless and in despair about how to break the news to me and my brothers.

Once they told us, I was sad, but mostly too much in shock and in denial to cry. It really did not hit me until we were at my grandmother's funeral and my father was reading her eulogy. I ran out of the church, crying uncontrollably.

I felt angry with my family and God because my grandmother was gone. I couldn't help but think about how she would never see me graduate from Penn State University or witness any other special moments in my future. It was very difficult for me. I saved her voicemail and would play repeatedly.

As time went by, I learned to adjust to the idea that my grandmother was truly gone and would not be back. Holidays, birthdays, Mother's Day, Easter, Summer—I knew things would be different. Slowly, I learned how to remember the joyous moments with my grandmother.

When you experience grief or loss, no one can tell you to just get over it or that time will heal all wounds. It is hard sometimes! You may feel as though no one knows how you are feeling and can't possibly experience the same pain and emotions you do.

Whenever in a moment of grief, take time to process how you feel. Use the moment to identify any memories that make you feel uneasy about the losses you experienced. It's important to label your feelings and create a list of ways you would like to use to cope with grief and loss.

Perhaps, you are not sure how you want people to support you but know that having a friend who will let you just cry and be in their presence may help. It is okay to acknowledge where you are in the grieving process and have a support group who will provide a safe space for you to process your emotions.

One of the difficult aspects of grief is the pain you experience. It can be hard to describe. When you are feeling pain, you can often feel isolated and like no one else understands. It is important to acknowledge the pain you are feeling to address how you will deal with it. I want you to know that I hear you and deeply understand the pain you are feeling. You have every right to have the feelings you have about your loss. It is truly hard. I want you to know that there are people to help you lighten your load as you walk this new journey.

Grief and Loss Activity

- Write a letter to the person you've lost about how you feel.

- Create a list of happy moments in your journal.

- Create a memory box with pictures, cards, gifts, items, etc. that reminds you of them and makes you feel happy.

- List the people in your support group you can reach out to when feeling distressed.

- Keep track of your sleeping patterns and eating habits.

Chapter 11: Harassment and Bullying

Dear Black Girl,

The Merriam-Webster dictionary defines bullying *as abuse or mistreatment of someone vulnerable by someone stronger and more powerful.* According to the National Center for Educational Statistics, 20.8% of students reported being bullied and 64% of children who are bullied do not report it at all. The study states that 24.7% of African-American students are bullied at school (U.S. Department of Education 2016).

Parents, bullying can occur directly or indirectly with your teen, whether in school or in other social settings. Bullying can affect your child in various ways, including isolation, shame, anxiety, depression, lack of social interaction with their peers and poor academic performance.

No one should get a pass for trying to harass you. Whether it happens at school or in your community, harassment is wrong. Harassment can take place in many forms, from sexual harassment to being cyberbullied by your peers.

Do you know how to identify and label what harassment looks like? You may have seen someone at school being harassed by another student but remained quiet and never said anything. Do you feel like it's not your business and you should just keep it moving? Let's talk about bullying— particularly cyberbullying.

The Internet is a powerful tool, but it is often used to do a lot of damage to the lives of teens. There have been countless stories of teens who deal with bullying from others on social media and in person. Bullying can either be cyber, emotional, verbal or physical abuse. If you see it happening, I want you to speak up about it.

Dear Parents,

Teens are told to walk away, tell an adult or ignore those who bully them. Some teens will respond with "whatever" and pretend the comments don't bother them at all. In reality, they may be internalizing what occurred. Here are some simple strategies to prevent your child from being bullied.

Look for warning signs

Look for changes in sleeping patterns, loss of appetite, change in moods and behavior. Also, look for changes in somatic symptoms, such as headaches and stomach pains. If you notice that something is different with your child, look for non-verbal cues. Many children struggle with how to tell their parents they are getting bullied, so it is important to look out for signs and talk to your child about bullying. Let them know it is okay for them to confide in you about this.

Know your facts about bullying

For parents, it may be difficult to hear that your child is being bullied. It is important to assess the type of bullying that is going on. Figure out if your child is being physically attacked and may be at risk for danger. Also assess if your child is being bullied verbally. Once you identify the type of bullying that is occurring, it is important to get school officials involved. Your child's school may offer a bullying prevention program.

Provide emotional support for your child

Empower your child through the process by being there to offer emotional support. Equip your child with problem solving and conflict resolution skills. Always tell your child that bullying is not their fault. Be a listening ear for your child and consider taking them to see a therapist for help learning calming skills to eliminate any overly emotional reactions.

Overall, bullying is not something to be ignored or dismissed. It can have long-term effects on your child, impacting their mood and behavior. It is important to learn strategies to prevent your child from being bullied and to help them build resilience.

Chapter 12: Teen Dating Violence

Dear Black Girl,

If you've ever been a victim of teen dating violence, it can impact how you view relationships in general. 1 in 3 teens will experience some form of teen dating abuse—and these abuses come in many forms. Types of dating violence include physical, emotional, and sexual abuse, stalking, financial abuse or even digital abuse.

Often, when people think of dating violence, they assume it involves only physical abuse that leaves marks and bruises on a person. However, there are cases where dating violence is not so noticeable to the naked eye. In these situations, you must be intentionally looking out for the warning signs of dating violence.

When it comes to dating violence, the perpetrator misuses their power and control to get you to feel powerless in the relationship. They may make you feel like you can't leave the relationship or continue life without them being there.

It's important to look for warning signs, such as name-calling, being isolated from your support system/tribe, or having your phone and whereabouts constantly being checked. Another warning sign is that the person is possessive and has a temper problem. If you are in a relationship and feel unsafe, you may want to think about whether the relationship is good for your mental health.

Perhaps you are not struggling with dating violence but know of a friend who is in a relationship with someone who constantly puts her in positions where she feels unsafe. Do not give up on this friend! Always check in to make sure she is okay. Safety should always be the number #1 priority. There will be times when you must seek guidance from an adult, trusted advisor or legal authority.

One of the forms of abuse that has grown over the years is digital abuse. Like cyberbullying, this is when a partner tries to control and monitor your usage of social media or technology. They may want access to all your social media accounts, have your passwords, and start an argument over who you follow on social media or who liked and commented on your page. They may also threaten to send your inappropriate images and "sexts" to others on social media.

Remember, never send nudes or inappropriate images to anyone and don't allow them to pressure you into doing something that you are not comfortable doing on social media. Maybe it's a little too late and you've already sent inappropriate images to someone on your phone. Try to see if you can get them to delete the images. You may run the risk of being a victim of child pornography and cause further legal issues due to inappropriate images of yourself being circulated around the internet.

Dating abuse is more common than many teens believe. Remember it is never your fault if it happens to you. Don't allow the shame and guilt of what happened to make you feel inferior to others. You are a conqueror and a survivor. You don't have to continue living in a repeated cycle of abuse. You can change the story you narrate in the future. You can work towards building a healthier relationship with someone who provides a space of peace and joy in your life.

You want a relationship where you can feel confident and not intimidated, safe and not harmed, appreciated and not judged, celebrated and not mocked, loved and not hated by them. Your relationship should push you closer to your future goals and not hinder the progress you've made so far in life. Take back your authority and your voice and walk out in your truths.

Chapter 13: Policing Black Girls

Dear Black Girl,

Metal detectors, school resource officers, suspension—you name it, you've probably seen it in your school or heard about the policing of Black girls in other schools. A study conducted by Monique Morris mentions that Black girls are 8 times more likely than White girls to be suspended from school (Morris 2016).

So, the question is "Why are we policing Black girls in school?" There isn't a simple answer to this question, but I do know that schools must do a better job of making sure that Black girls feel safe in school. For Black girls, there are so many misconceptions—about being "too loud," "too ghetto," and "too angry." This isn't a positive image and it can become extremely frustrating to exercise your rights and express your feelings in a space that makes you feel unheard or unsafe.

With the rise in school shootings, metal detectors and school resource officers were installed in schools as a safety measure, so students couldn't bring in weapons or contraband. However, when you enter a school and immediately face a metal detector beeping as you go through it, one can't help but wonder if they were placed there to make you feel safer, or if the school simply does not provide a sense of safety and instead makes you feel like a prisoner.

Aside from metal detectors, the physical presence of a school resource officer (A.K.A security with armed weapons) can cause you to feel triggered in a school setting. There have been countless stories of Black girls being removed from their classrooms by officers or forcefully mishandled by an adult or authority figure in schools and community settings.

Outside of school settings, you may have heard many other stories in the media about Black girls who are policed or pushed into the criminal justice system. When I speak to Black girls, I often ask them if their view of police officers have changed over the years, due to what is happening in our political climate. If you feel ill towards law enforcement, I encourage you to explore and process those feelings.

Don't allow anyone to make you feel like your feelings are invalid. Take time to understand how vicarious trauma, racial trauma, and systemic racism may play a role. The role of local law enforcement in your community is to make sure that you feel safe when there is an emergency. Perhaps, your local authority needs to do cultural competency training to learn how to effectively work with girls of color.

Chapter 14:

Black Girls, Politics, and Civic

Engagement

Dear Black Girl,

Did you know that there has been an increase in the number of women—particularly minority women—in politics? Over the years, teens have expressed growing interest in politics, advocacy, and civic engagement. When you get involved in politics, you can exercise more of your rights and make your voice heard regarding your concerns with issues in your community, globally and internationally.

When I was five years old, my dad would bring me to political protests in Brooklyn, New York to see how the protests were organized regarding Haitian politics. I did not understand what was going on and was confused by the passion in people's eyes, the anger in their voices, and the police officers on the sidelines ready to charge if they saw anything that seemed "aggressive" in their eyes.

I did not gain any interest in politics until my adult years, after witnessing the mistreatment of brown and Black kids by police officers and the policies being created that did not protect minority youth. I did not know much about politics or where to start, so I started volunteering through canvassing and dropping off campaign brochures at people's doors in my community.

My aim was to get them to vote for a particular councilwoman in my city. It felt good to volunteer in a city that I loved for a councilwoman who wanted to bring changes to our educational system for youths. I continued to attend events related to policy and leadership to develop the skills I needed to not only be a better therapist, but also advocate for teen girls.

You now live in a generation where you have access to various organizations, hashtags, and campaigns right from your phone. If you feel a strong need to get involved in politics and advocacy, then I suggest you investigate ways to ways to push the right narratives and your message within your community using the platforms you've been given.

Whether you choose to get involved in student council, participate in a mock trial team, or join a local youth council committee, you can learn ways to advocate for what you believe. Remember, you are a leader. The world needs to hear the deep desires and passions of your heart. The change begins with you.

Chapter 15:

Where are the Black Girls in my School?

Dear Black Girl,

I know the feeling all too well, of being the only Black girl or one of a tiny handful of Black students at your school. I grew up attending a mostly Black primary school in Newark, NJ, but when I started middle school, I was sent to a very small private school in Livingston, NJ, a primarily white neighborhood. After that, I went on to attend high school in a rural community in Pennsylvania. There again, the demographic of my school was mostly white. It was different.

I had to adjust to my new school and my new community that had no streetlights, no bodegas, and deer were like neighbors. There were cultural differences I had to deal with, such as people asking, "Can I touch your hair?" or repeatedly having to explain to my Caucasian friends why my Haitian parents wouldn't allow me to date until I finished college (just kidding...not really). Sometimes, I would come home feeling extremely frustrated that my parents sent me to a school where I felt like the minority. They did not understand what I was going through.

I am sure you can relate to attending a school where you feel like no one understands you. Do you ever feel like you must "code switch" in school? Code switching is the act of switching the voice you use depending on who is around you. You may put on your "white speaking voice" or feel like you must decide who you really are when you go back home and hang out with your Black friends.

Sometimes, you may feel like you aren't "Black enough" for your Black friends and are "too Black" for your white friends. Maybe you've heard people say, "you sound like a white girl," as if you aren't allowed to speak in a certain manner. It is a real struggle when you want to build friendships but feel like you can't be who you really are around your peers. It's important to not lose your identity during your teenage years. Find those friends who will appreciate you for who you are too.

Something else that may be frustrating is living in America as a Black girl and watching events in the media that impact you or your community. It may feel like some of your peers do not understand what you're going through or the significance of #BlackLivesMatter. It can be emotionally draining for you to want to fight for justice but feel stuck between two worlds.

Another challenge that girls of color face is having to validate their experiences and fight for their positions in predominantly white spaces. No matter how smart you are, it may feel like you must fight harder for awards, leadership positions, honor societies, and admissions into ivy league schools. It can often seem like your counterparts work less than you do, but get the awards, accolades, and affirmations from educational institutions.

Remember, the measure of your greatness is not determined by those who don't see you or reward your greatness. It is up to you to continue to see the value you possess and can offer to this world. From high school to college to the workplace, you will experience these behaviors towards women of color. When you attend a school where most other students do not look like you, it can be hard to find your identity in those spaces. I want to encourage you by saying this: DO NOT SHRINK who you are to fit in with other students.

I want you to gradually flow into who you are and show them your Black girl magic! Think of activities you can do in the community that make you feel free to flow in your gifts. Whether it be the Girl Scouts, Boys and Girls Club, Jack and Jill, NAACP, church youth groups, etc.

Consider starting a club at your school that will help you to build your identity and cultural competence.

Activity

The purpose of the activity is to help you create safe spaces within your school, so you feel like you belong and matter.

- Name some extracurricular activities you enjoy at school.

- What activities/clubs do you wish your school offered?

- What are some clubs you can create at your school?

- Name 3 ways you can build social relationships with other kids in your school.

Name 10 things you love about your school.

_____

_____

_____

_____

_____

_____

_____

_____

_____

_____

_____

_____

_____

_____

_____

_____

_____

_____

_____

_____

_____

_____

What are some things you wish the other students knew about your culture and identity?

Chapter 16:

College Planning and Goal Setting

Dear Black Girl,

I always knew I wanted to attend college, but I did not take the college application process seriously. I wanted to enjoy my high school experience, as I knew that soon, we would all venture off to new states and cities. Despite having a high GPA throughout most of my childhood and teenage years, I "successfully" failed at taking standardized tests. When I took the SATs, I believe I had the lowest score in the entire high school. I am embarrassed to say this, but I had a 650 on the SATs (I know, that's pretty bad). Once I received my scores, I started to stress out and panic. I doubted that I would ever get into my #1 school choice—Penn State University.

By the grace of God, I got into Penn State and received a partial scholarship. By no means am I telling you to not study for the SATs or just ignore achieving academic success in high school. My journey to getting into college does not have to be your story. You can properly prepare and plan to get into college without increasing your stress levels.

As a therapist, I have worked with hundreds of teens, just like you, who wonder "what's next?" once high school is over. I have worked with teens who are overwhelmed with stress, anxiety, or comparison during this time in high school. There are times when you may feel frustrated with the process and sit by watching your friends receive acceptance letters and full-ride scholarships to top schools. As you wait your turn, this can lead to comparisons and, for some, jealousy.

If you are considering attending college, this may be one of the most stressful moments of your high school career. From the application process to the waiting game to receiving college acceptance letters, it is important to mentally prepare for each possible outcome. I will offer some strategies and tips to help you get through the process.

Grab a Journal

Have a journal dedicated to the college planning and application process. You will use this planner to jot down your ideas, your dream schools, ideas for majors, open houses, deadlines, etc. This journal will also serve as a memory for when you get into college and want to look back at all the hard work you've put in. Use the journal to write down your fears, but also create a manifestation section that you can visualize your vision and dreams.

Talk to your Guidance Counselor

Reach out to your guidance counselor to map out your projected plans post-high school. If you plan on attending college, ask your guidance counselor about potential scholarships, information on college open houses, SAT prep classes, and assistance with completing your application packet. If you don't plan on attending college, talk to your guidance counselor about alternative options, such as joining the military, attending trade school, or obtaining a job. It is important to get as many resources as you can from your guidance counselor before you graduate.

Create a Vision Board

You can create a vision board using magazines, poster board, glue, and scissors to visualize your future goals. Another option is to create a SMART GOALS list. SMART goals stand for **S**pecific, **M**easurable, **A**ttainable, **R**ealistic, and **T**imely. When you center your goals around the SMART formula, this allows you to set goals that are realistic. You can also create goals that are short-term and long-term.

Chapter 17: Healing After a Heartbreak

Dear Black Girl,

Breakups suck! Whether it was your decision to break up or their decision to end the relationship, it can be difficult to start a new norm when the relationship is over. You are faced with questions like "what happened?" and "why did you guys break up?" and a multitude of others thrown your way by your family and friends. Listen, if the break up was hard, then please take your time to process how you feel about the relationship ending. Acknowledge any feelings of hurt, heartbreak, rejection, and embarrassment. Maybe you feel overjoyed and at peace that it's over and you can move back to your normal life without the stressors of dating someone.

Sometimes, girls will say, "I don't care if it's over" rather than express their true emotions and feelings. Some girls find themselves becoming guarded and unable to be vulnerable with those around them. Maybe you feel like you must act like you don't care because your old boo moved on to a new boo and you don't want to act like you still have feelings for your old boo. I get it, it's hard. But what happens when you go home late at night, and you're in your room, and you start thinking about how the breakup has impacted or affected your mood?

Maybe it's in that moment, when you are scrolling on Instagram and you see they've posted new pictures with their new #BAE. You see all the people who like the photo and are commenting "#Goals...."YASSSSS" and leaving heart emojis under the picture. It can leave you feeling stressed and hurt that someone did not have the same feelings for you in the relationship. Maybe you constantly play back the thoughts in your mind about where the relationship went wrong. Maybe you are comparing yourself to their new girlfriend.

Relationships and breakups can get super complicated. If you don't learn how to fully process your emotions during the experience, you may find yourself in a new relationship that leaves you feeling stressed out once again.

After breaking up, take your time to learn how to fill the gap with other things. Often, when you break up with someone, you may go through a period where you miss them and are not sure how to fill in your time without having to FaceTime, text or meet up in person. During this transition period, learn how to create happy moments with yourself: whether it's a new hobby, spending more time with your siblings, staying on track with your homework assignments or completing household chores.

Now that the relationship is over, ask yourself who are you following on social media. You may need to consider placing boundaries around your social media usage and determining if it's healthy to follow your ex. Sometimes, the people you follow on social media can make a break up harder on you as you navigate this new space, especially if you are feeling lonely.

Choose to unfollow, unfriend, or block as you need to, or even consider taking social media break to lessen any additional stressors. You can use this time to fuel your efforts to create social engagement offline with your family and friends. Remember that during a break up it is necessary for you to take care of yourself and your heart, because you matter.

Chapter 18: Self-Care and Black Girls

Dear Black Girl,

Do you know what self-care is? When was the last time you practiced self-care? Self-care is the practice of preserving your own mental health. I don't want you to think that self-care is something that only adults indulge in. This is something you can do to preserve your emotional and mental health. The purpose of self-care is to learn to say YES to yourself more often.

Life can be extremely stressful and busy, but it's important to set boundaries and guidelines for yourself. You will be pulled in many directions by school, family, friends, lovers and more. You must learn how to create moments of self-care, so you can practice self-love. There are several types of self-care which we will discuss in this chapter, including emotional, social, physical, psychological, financial and spiritual self-care. To effectively practice self-care, you will have to learn its various elements.

Emotional Self-Care

This helps you to recognize your emotions and properly process what you are feeling. You can do this through journaling your thoughts or talking to someone about your feelings. According to a research study done by Glasgow University, there are 6 basic emotions: happiness, sadness, fear, anger, surprise, and disgust (*Written All Over Your Face*). One thing I have learned from working with teens is that they sometimes struggle to identify their emotions and use additional words related to their emotions.

Social Self-Care

This is where you make an intentional effort to hang out with your friends. It is important to build relationships with your friends and family. However, make sure you are not on your phone the entire time that you are supposed to be hanging out. Social self-care is a way to grow relationships beyond the "how are you doing?" and "I'm fine" moments. This is a chance for you to ask yourself and your friends how they are doing and learn more about the deepest desires of their hearts. This is an opportunity to learn how you can receive the support you are looking for from your friends. To learn more about relationship building, think about the common interests and goals you have with your friends. Some common interests and goals can be things like attending concerts, volunteering, painting, and learning new dances together. This allows you to do team building activities and learn how to laugh together without the use of your phone.

Physical Self-Care

You've probably heard people saying, "drink water and mind your business." This statement has some truth to it. Practicing physical self-care means you will learn how to practice healthy habits and take care of your body. This is where you show up for yourself first, whether it's through getting more rest, eating healthy, exercising or drinking more water.

Sleep

Rest is extremely important during your adolescent years. Studies have shown that adolescents need between 8.5-10 hours of rest each night (National Sleep Foundation). In my many years of working with teens, many have stated that they get less than the required amount of sleep they need each night. One benefit of getting a good night's rest is that the chemicals in your body will be allowed to do their job. This allows your brain to get rest and allows your brain to store the memory it needs.

When you lack rest, you may notice a shift in your mood and attention span. I have heard from many teens who sleep late, due to homework or spending time on their phone, that this can become problematic. I want you to start tracking how much time you spend getting rest. In addition, consider practicing sleep hygiene (see Appendix). Sleep hygiene is a daily practice that will teach your body how to rest and relax.

Eating Healthy Foods

Pizza and lattes may not be the healthiest choices of food. Did you know that, even as a teenager, the meals you eat may contribute to some of your stress levels and how you feel emotionally during the day? To adjust your health, you will have to change some of the foods you decide to eat. Consider adding more foods that improve brain health, such as avocados, almonds, dark chocolates, fish, blueberries, turmeric, oranges, green tea, and pumpkin seeds.

Exercising

Whether you have access to a gym or not, you can find ways to stay active. You may even consider joining a sports team or club at your school to stay active. Staying active as a teen helps with concentration and allows endorphins to keep your mood happy.

Psychological Self-Care

This is difficult for many teens to do. It requires you to engage in self-reflection. Sometimes, we are the causes of our own stressors by putting too much on our plates and not learning how to set boundaries with the people around us. If you struggle with saying no to your friends and are always concerned with pleasing them, then you may find yourself in many situations that stress you out. You must learn how to pay attention to your thoughts, feelings, moods, and behaviors. This will be a moment for you to learn how to practice journaling or setting boundaries with those around you.

Financial Self-Care

Before you can secure the bag, it is important for you to learn how to manage your finances. Even though you may be an adolescent, this is a time when you might be getting your first job or entering the employment market after high school. I remember when I was in high school and received my first paycheck. The first thing I purchased was a curling iron for my hair. I was left with $0 the same day I received my paycheck.

From that moment, I spent every dollar I earned in high school on the latest fashion trends, fancy nail art, buying my friends' lunches, and shoes. This behavior pattern continued through college. I slowly learned how much of a horrible steward of my finances I had been when I encountered real bills, such as college book fees, rent, and credit card payments. While you may be a teenager and feel like you don't have adult responsibilities, this will be a great time for you to learn how to be disciplined with your finances and practice healthy habits. You can start with opening a savings account, with the help of a parent or legal guardian. After that, you can start saving a portion of your finances, allowances, and money received from gifts.

Spiritual Self-Care

This is more than just praying and going to church. When we hear the word spiritual, we often associate it with God. I want you to go beyond looking at spiritual well-being as just being about going to church and praying. Ask yourself, when was the last time you asked for forgiveness? When was the last time you offered to volunteer or give to someone in need? When was the last time you put feelings of jealousy to the side to congratulate someone who received the same blessing you were praying for?

Spiritual self-care requires self-reflection, to observe the condition of your heart at this moment. One of my favorite scriptures in the Bible is Galatians 5:22. It says, "but the fruit of the Spirit is love, joy, peace, forbearance, kindness, goodness, faithfulness, gentleness, and self-control."

When you look at these words, do you feel they represent who you are? If so, ask yourself how you can make improvements to practice the Fruit of the Spirit daily in your life. If you feel like there is an area you need to work on, ask yourself how you can make those changes to do better.

Although I grew up in a Christian household, I did not feel I had a close relationship with God during my teenage years. It wasn't until my mid-20s that I developed a strong relationship with God. Some of the spiritual self-care practices I had to develop included learning how to be vulnerable with my prayers, practicing gratitude daily, and learning to be patient with others. I also had to learn to be content and not compare myself to others on social media. I learned to forgive those who offended me and how to give grace to others and not be judgmental.

Chapter 19: The Black Girl Affirmation

Dear Black Girl,

I am a Black girl. I am amazing.

I stand tall as I walk through this crooked world that seems to forget who I am sometimes.

I link arms with the women who come before me and who will come after me to show my sisterhood.

I am powerful.

I can have positive relationships in my life.

I am hopeful.

I am peaceful. I am loved and give love.

I acknowledge everything that has caused me pain and flip it into something good.

I am always a student, but a teacher to many.

I deserve every dream that I desire, and it will come into fruition.

I am breaking every generational curse that tried to stop me from my purpose.

I am birthing a legacy that will be left for my children's children. I am fearfully and wonderfully made in the image of God.

I am a force to be reckoned with and my voice will shake things up in this nation for the better.

I am BLACK GIRL MAGIC.

About the Author

Marline Francois-Madden is the owner of Hearts Empowerment Counseling Center, a contributor to the Huffington Post, and a phenomenal public speaker and entrepreneur. With over 15 years of clinical experience, she has become a sought-after expert in mental health, trauma, self-care and girls' leadership. Marline has shared her expertise at dozens of universities, colleges, community organizations, churches and conferences— including the Congressional Black Caucus for Women and Girls.

Her organization, Far More Precious, has awarded $2,500 in scholarships to minority girls since 2013 and it continues to educate young women between ages 14-19 to dream beyond the barriers they face to reach their fullest potential. She was named a Nominated Changemaker by the White House at the State of the Women summit during President Obama's administration. Her work has been featured on HuffPost, Hot

97, Fox5, Bustle, Business Insider, Elite Daily, Psych Central and various other media platforms.

Empowerment isn't what she does, it's who she is.

Driven by passion and purpose, Marline touches the lives of many through her work. She facilitated trauma-informed group and individual sessions for young women in Haiti who were survivors of sex trafficking. Her commitment to youth development earned her an invite to speak to young global leaders from countries such as Pakistan, Nigeria, Kenya, Israel, and Bangladesh about self-care. She also volunteered at a children's orphanage in Ghana.

Conscious of living what she teaches, Marline believes that everyone can live a life of service and be intentional about self-care: the two are not mutually exclusive. She continues to be a pillar of leadership in her work as a coach for mental health professionals who seek to expand their expertise, brand themselves, and diversify their income.

Marline has a bachelor's degree in Psychology from Penn State University and a master's degree in Social Work from Rutgers University-Newark. She is the Chair of the National Association of Social Workers' Legislative and Social Action committee and she serves on various non-profit boards, while remaining actively involved in mentoring youth. She is also a Licensed Clinical Social Worker in the state of New Jersey. Marline resides in New Jersey with her husband.

To learn more about Marline, please check out her website at www.marlinefrancois.com

To learn more about The State of Black Girls programs, please check us out at www.thestateofblackgirls.com

For information on how to book Marline to speak at your next event, please email her at info@marlinefrancois.com.

If you are interested in booking wellness programs or consultation services, please check out our website at www.thestateofblackgirls.com.

Appendix A - List of Emotions

Amazed	Angry	Annoyed	Ashamed	Bitter
Bored	Compassionate	Comfortable	Confused	Content
Curious	Delighted	Determined	Disdain	Disgusted
Depressed	Eager	Embarrassed	Energetic	Envious
Excited	Exhilarated	Foolish	Frustrated	Furious
Grieving	Guilty	Happy	Hopeful	Humiliated
Hurt	Inadequate	Insecure	Inspired	Irritated
Jealous	Joy	Lonely	Lost	Loving
Melancholy	Miserable	Motivated	Neglected	Nervous
Optimistic	Overwhelmed	Peaceful	Proud	Regretful
Relieved	Resentful	Sad	Satisfied	Scared
Self-conscious	Shocked	Silly	Stupid	Suspicious
Trapped	Tense	Terrified	Uncomfortable	Worried

Appendix B - Teen Awareness Month

January

January 11:

National Human Trafficking Awareness Day

National Mentoring Month

February

Black History Month

Teen Dating Violence Awareness Month

March

National Women's History Month

National Women and Girls HIV/AIDS Awareness Day
(March 10)

April

Teen Health Week (April 1 - 7)

World Autism Awareness Day

Child Abuse Prevention Month

Sexual Assault Awareness and Prevention Month

National Youth Prevention Violence Week

(April 8 -13)

National Youth HIV/AIDS Awareness Day

(April 10)

Take Our Daughters and Sons to Work Day

(April 27)

May

National Teen Pregnancy Awareness Month

Mental Health Awareness Month

June

PTSD Awareness Month

LGBT Awareness Month

National HIV Testing Day (June 27)

July

National Minority Awareness Month

August

National Friendship Day (August 4th)

September

Suicide Prevention Week (September 8-14)

Sexual Health Month

Childhood Cancer Awareness Month

October

National Bullying Prevention Month

National Substance Abuse Awareness Month

Mental Health Awareness Week (October 6-12)

November

Adoption Awareness Month

December

World AIDS Day (December 1)

Appendix C - Coping Skills List

- Create your favorite playlist.

- Take a hot bath.

- Dance.

- Sing.

- Play your favorite instrument.

- Cry.

- Talk to a friend.

- Paint your nails..

- Light some candles and listen to your favorite song that uplifts your spirits.

- Journal your thoughts on paper.

- Write a poem.

- Say a prayer.

- List 10 things you are grateful for this week.

- Tell someone "I love you".

- Tell someone "I forgive you".

- Go for a walk in the park.

- Do five different outdoor activities, like hiking, riding your bike, running, etc.

- Have a picnic with your girlfriends.

- Talk to a friend about what's stressing you out.

- Take some selfies and post an affirmation about yourself on social media.

- Create a vision board.

- Go shopping with a close friend or relative.

- Volunteer at a soup kitchen, nursing home, or local animal shelter.

- Meditate and practice some deep breathing exercises.

- Tell yourself it's going to be okay.

- Watch a movie that makes you laugh until you cry.

- Take a nap.

- Snuggle up with your teddy bear or a loved one.

- Give someone a long hug that you love.

Appendix D - 10 Ways to Journal

1. Create a list of your wins and celebrate yourself.

2. Create a list of affirmations about yourself.

3. Write down your goals and dreams for this year and/or your future.

4. Write out your daily thoughts and keep track of your emotions.

5. Create a list of things you are grateful for each day.

6. Create a list of fun, childhood memories, so you never forget to tap into your inner child.

7. Create a bucket list of things you'd like to accomplish. Write down your experiences.

8. Create a list of inspiration and motivational quotes.

9. Reflect on an experience that has changed your life and write it down.

10. Write down your fears and create a list of how you plan to overcome each fear.

Bibliography

1. *Blake, Jamilia J., Thalia González, and Rebecca Epstein.* "Girlhood Interrupted: The Erasure of Black Girls' Childhood." The Center on Poverty and Inequality. Georgetown Law Center, 2017. Web.

2. *Girls and Teens | Anxiety and Depression Association of America, ADAA.* https://adaa.org/find-help-for/women/mental-health-in-young-girls-and-teens.

3. *Child Abuse Statistics.* http://www.cactn.org/child-abuse-information/statistics.

4. *"Student Reports of Bullying: Results From the 2015 School Crime Supplement to the National Crime Victimization Survey."* Student Reports of Bullying, U.S. Department of Education, Dec. 2016, nces.ed.gov/pubs2017/2017015.pdf

5. *Morris, Monique W. "Pushout."* Pushout: The Criminalization of Black Girls in Schools. The New Press (2016). Web.

6. *Written All over Your Face: Humans Express Four Basic Emotions Rather than Six, Says New Study.* https://www.gla.ac.uk/news/archiveofnews/2014/february/headline_306019_en.html.

7. *"Sleep for Teenagers* - National Sleep Foundation." *Sleep for Teenagers*, https://www.sleepfoundation.org/articles/teens-and-sleep.

8. *"11 Facts About Teens and Self Esteem."* DoSomething.Org, https://www.dosomething.org/us/facts/11-facts-about-teens-and-self-esteem.

Made in the USA
Middletown, DE
16 January 2020